Table of Conte

Crazy Crocodile Afghan
page 6

Westphalia Afghan,
page 14

Dragonslayer Afghan,
page 21

Belle Fleur Baby Afghan

Skill Level
 ■■■☐ INTERMEDIATE

Finished Measurements
35 inches wide × 42 inches long

Materials
- Berroco Comfort DK light (DK) weight acrylic/nylon yarn (1¾ oz/178 yds/50g per skein):
  7 skeins #2702 pearl
  4 skeins each #2719 sunshine and #2740 seedling
- Size G/6/4mm crochet hook or size needed to obtain gauge
- Stitch marker
- Tapestry needle

3 LIGHT

Gauge
19 dc = 4 inches; 10 dc rnds = 4 inches

Pattern Notes
Some rounds are crocheted after turning the work; take note of the right-side and wrong-side designations.

Join with slip stitch as indicated unless otherwise stated.

Chain-3 at beginning of round counts as first double crochet unless otherwise stated.

Special Stitches
Sideways slip stitch (sslst): Insert hook under front lp of indicated st and immediately under

Front Loop & Side

front vertical lp of same st *(see illustration)*, yo, draw through all lps on hook.

Sideways single crochet (ssc): Insert hook under front lp of st just made and immediately under front vertical lp of same st *(see previous illustration)*, yo, pull up lp, yo, draw through both lps on hook.

Picot: Ch 2, **ssc** *(see Special Stitches)* in side of st at base of ch-2.

Crocodile petal (petal): (5 dc, **picot**—*see Special Stitches*, 5 dc) in indicated sp.

Crocodile leaf (leaf): (Tr, 5 dc, picot, 5 dc, tr) in indicated sp.

Tack: Insert hook in picot of next row 5 petal and then in next row 9 sc, yo, draw through both layers, yo, draw through rem lps on hook.

Afghan

Block A
Make 26.

Rnd 1 (WS): With pearl, make **slip ring** *(see illustration)* and work 8 sc in ring, **join** *(see Pattern Notes)* in first sc, tighten ring. *(8 sc)*

Rnd 2: Ch 1, (sc, tr) in each of next 8 sc, join in first sc. *(16 sts)*

4" end

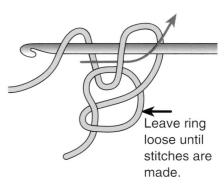
Leave ring loose until stitches are made.

Slip Ring

Note: The tr sts will naturally pop out on the WS of the fabric. For the purposes of this pattern, the "bumpy" side will be considered the RS of the fabric.

Rnd 3: Ch 1, (sc, tr) in same st, (sc, tr) in each of next 15 sts, join in first st. Fasten off. *(32 sts)*

Rnd 4: Join sunshine with sc in any sc, ch 6, **sslst** *(see Special Stitches)* in sc at base of ch, (sc, tr, sc) in next sc, [sc in next sc, ch 6, sslst in sc at base of ch, (sc, tr, sc) in next sc] 7 times, join in first sc, turn. *(8 ch-6 sps, 8 tr, 16 sc)*

Rnd 5 (RS): Ch 1, [sc in next tr, **petal** *(see Special Stitches)* in next ch-6 sp] 8 times, sl st in first sc to join, turn. *(8 petals)*

Rnd 6 (WS): [Ch 3, fold petal away, sc in row 4 st at center of next petal, ch 3, sc in sc between current and next petal] 8 times, join in first ch-3. Fasten off. *(16 ch-3 sps, 16 sc)*

Rnd 7 (WS): Join seedling with sc in any sc behind a petal, *3 sc in next ch-3 sp, sc in next sc, ch 6, sslst in sc at base of ch, 3 sc in next ch-3 sp**, sc in next sc, rep from * around, ending last rep at **, join in first sc, turn. *(8 ch-6 sps, 56 sc)*

Rnd 8 (RS): Ch 1, [**leaf** *(see Special Stitches)* in next ch-6 sp, sk 3 sc, sc in next sc] 8 times, join in first ch, turn. *(8 petals, 8 sc)*

Rnd 9 (WS): Ch 1, [sc in next sc, ch 4, fold next leaf away, dc in st at center of leaf, ch 4, sc in next sc, ch 4, fold next leaf away, sc in st at center of leaf, ch 4] 4 times, join in first sc, turn. Counting backwards, place marker in 2nd ch-4 sp from join. Fasten off. *(4 dc, 12 sc, 16 ch-4 sps)*

Rnd 10 (RS): With pearl, join with dc in marked sp, ch 2, *(2 dc, 2 hdc, sc) in next ch-4 sp, **tack** *(see Special Stitches)*, 3 sc in next ch-4 sp, sk next sc, 3 sc in next ch-4 sp, tack, (sc, 2 hdc**, 2 dc) in next ch-4 sp, ch 2, rep from * around, ending last rep at **, dc in same ch-4 sp, join in first dc, sl st in ch-2 sp, do not turn. *(72 sts, 4 corner ch sps)*

Rnd 11: Ch 3 *(see Pattern Notes)*, (dc, ch 2, 2 dc) in same sp, *dc in each of next 18 sts**, (2 dc, ch 2, 2 dc) in next ch-2 corner sp, rep from * around, ending last rep at **, join in top of ch-3. *(88 sts, 4 corner ch sps)*

Rnd 12: Sl st in next dc, sl st in next ch-2 sp, ch 1, [(sc, ch 2, sc) in next ch-2 sp, sc in **back lp** *(see Stitch Guide)* of each of next 22 dc] 4 times, join in first sc. *(96 sc, 4 ch sps)*

Rnd 13: Sl st in next sc, sl st in ch sp, ch 3, (dc, ch 2, 2 dc) in same sp, *dc in back lp of each of next 24 sc**, (2 dc, ch 2, 2 dc) in next ch sp, rep from * around, ending last rep at **, join in top of ch-3. Fasten off. *(104 sts, 4 ch sps)*

Block B
Make 4.

Work rnds 1–3 of Block A with sunshine.

Work rnds 4–6 of Block A with pearl.

Work rnds 7–13 of Block A with seedling.

Assembly
Weave in all ends.

Strip 1
Make 4.

With RS tog and pearl, using sl st seam, join 5 A Blocks in a row.

Strip 2
Make 2.

With RS tog and pearl, using sl st seam, join alternating Blocks A–B–A–B–A in a row.

Square

Join Strips in following order: 1–2–1–1–2–1.

Edging

Rnd 1: With RS facing, working across short end of Afghan, join pearl with sc in corner ch sp, (ch 2, sc) in same sp, sc in back lp of each of next 29 sts, [2 sc in sl st join between Blocks, sc in back lp of each of next 30 sts] 3 times, (ch 2, sc) in same ch-2 corner sp as last sc, sc in back lp of each of next 29 sts, rep between [ ] 6 times, (ch 2, sc) in same ch-2 corner sp as last sc, sc in back lp of each of next 29 sts, rep between [ ] 5 times, (ch 2, sc) in same ch-2 corner sp as last sc, sc in back lp of each of next 29 sts, rep between [ ] 5 times, 2 sc in sl st join between Blocks, sc in back lp of each of next 28 sts, place marker in sc just made, sc in last st, join in first sc. Fasten off. *(160 sts along each short side, 192 sts along each long side)*

Rnd 2: With sunshine, join with hdc in marked st, hdc in each of next 2 sts, (hdc, ch 6, sslst in hdc at base of ch, hdc) in ch-2 corner sp, place marker in ch-6 sp just made, hdc in each of next 7 sts, *ch 6, sslst in hdc at base of ch, hdc in each of next 8 sts*, rep between * 18 times, (ch 6, sslst in hdc at base of ch, hdc) in same ch-2 corner sp as last hdc, hdc in each of next 7 sts, repeat between * 23 times, (ch 6, sslst in hdc at base of ch, hdc) in same ch-2 corner sp as last hdc, hdc in each of next 7 sts, rep between * 19 times, (ch 6, sslst in hdc at base of ch, hdc) in same ch-2 corner sp as last hdc, hdc in each of next 7 sts, rep between * 22 times, ch 6, sslst in hdc at base of ch, hdc in each of next 4 sts, join in first hdc. *(160 hdc, 19 ch-6 sps on each short side, 192 hdc and 23 ch-6 sps on each long side, 4 ch-6 corner lps)*

Rnd 3: Ch 1, sc in same st, sk next 2 hdc, leaf in next ch-6 corner sp, sk next 2 hdc, sc in next hdc, ch 6, ssc in sc at base of ch, sc in next hdc, *petal in next ch-6 sp, sk next 2 hdc, sc in next hdc, ch 6, ssc in sc at base of ch, sc in next hdc*, rep between * 18 times, leaf in next ch-6 corner sp, sk next 2 hdc, sc in next hdc, ch 6, ssc in sc at base of ch, sc in next hdc, rep between * 23 times, leaf in next ch-6 corner sp, sk next 2 hdc, sc in next hdc, ch 6, ssc in sc at base of ch, sc in next hdc, rep between * 19 times, leaf in next ch-6 corner lp, sk next 2 hdc, sc in next hdc, ch 6, ssc in sc at base of ch, sc in next hdc, rep between * 22 times, petal in next ch-6 sp, sk next 2 hdc, sc in next hdc, ch 6, ssc in sc at base of ch, join in first sc. Fasten off. *(19 petals, 20 ch-6 sps on each short side, 23 petals and 24 ch-6 sps on each long side, 4 corner leaves).*

Rnd 4: With seedling, join with tr in any ch-6 sp, (5 dc, picot, 5 dc, tr) in same ch-6 sp, fold next petal forward, insert hook through **back strands** *(see illustration)* of first st at center of petal, yo and pull through st, yo and pull through both lps on hook, sc in back strands of next st at center of petal, *leaf in next ch-6 sp, sc in back strands of each of next 2 sts at center of petal*, rep between * 82 times, join in first tr. Fasten off. *(88 leaves, 176 sc)*

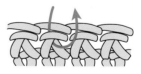

Back strands of SC

Finishing

Weave in ends. ●

Crazy Crocodile Afghan

Skill Level

 INTERMEDIATE

Finished Measurements

36 inches wide × 48 inches long

Materials

4
MEDIUM

- Berroco Comfort medium (worsted) weight acrylic/nylon yarn (3½ oz/210 yds/100g per skein):
  6 skeins each #9728 raspberry sorbet, #9717 raspberry coulis and #9789 cranberry heather
- Size H/8/5mm crochet hook or size needed to obtain gauge
- Stitch markers
- Tapestry needle

Gauge

5 rows of Diagonal Shell pattern = 3 inches along each straight edge

Pattern Notes

This piece is worked in **Diagonal Shell pattern** *(see illustration)* and starts in 1 corner and widens to form a triangle.

Upon reaching desired width, the number of clusters is decreased to form a rectangle.

Crocodile stitch edging is worked last.

When working the scales row, the piece is turned back and forth to work scales on right side and anchor stitches on wrong side.

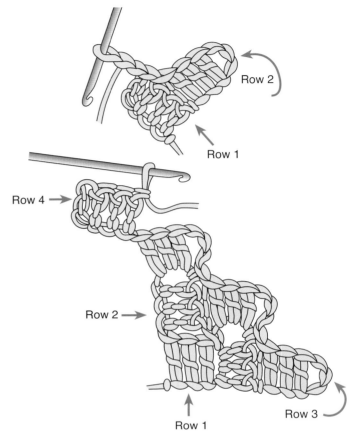

Diagonal Shell

Special Stitches

Sideways single crochet (ssc): Insert hook under front lp of st just made and immediately under front vertical lp of same st *(see illustration)*, yo, pull up lp, yo, draw through both lps on hook.

Front Loop & Side

Picot: Ch 2, **ssc** *(see Special Stitches)* in side of st at base of ch-2.

Afghan

Center Block

Row 1 (corner row): With sorbet, ch 6, dc **in back bar** *(see illustration)* of 4th ch from hook and in each of next 2 chs.

Back Bar of Chain

Row 2 (first inc): Ch 6, dc in back bar of 4th ch from hook and each of next 2 ch, turn by flipping the corner row up *(see Diagonal Shell pattern in Pattern Notes)*, sc in ch-3 sp from row 1, ch 2, 3 dc in same ch-2 sp.

Row 3: Ch 6, dc in back bar of 4th ch from hook and in each of the next 2 ch, flip corner up, [sc in next ch-2 sp from previous row, ch 2, 3 dc in same ch-2 sp] 2 times.

Row 4 (inc row): Ch 6, dc in back bar of 4th ch from hook and in each of the next 2 ch, flip corner up, [sc in next ch-2 sp from previous row, ch 2, 3 dc in same ch-2 sp] across.

Rows 5–10: Rep row 4. At end of row 10, **change color** *(see Stitch Guide)* to coulis.

Rows 11–20: With coulis, rep row 4. At end of row 20, change to cranberry.

Rows 21–30: With cranberry, rep row 4. At end of row 30, change to sorbet.

Rows 31–40: With sorbet, rep row 4. At end of row 40, change to coulis.

Rows 41–50: With coulis, rep row 4. At end of row 50, change to cranberry.

Rows 51–60: With cranberry, rep row 4. At end of row 60, turn.

Row 61: Ch 3, sc in ch-2 sp from previous row, change to sorbet on last yo and pull through, [ch 2, 3 dc in same ch-2 sp, sc in next ch-2 sp from previous row] across, turn.

Rows 62–70: Ch 3, sc in ch-2 sp from previous row, [ch 2, 3 dc in same ch-2 sp, sc in next ch-2 sp from previous row] across, turn.

Row 71: Ch 3, sc in ch-2 sp from previous row, change to coulis on last yo and pull through, [ch 2, 3 dc in same ch-2 sp, sc in next ch-2 sp from previous row] across, turn.

Rows 72–80: Rep row 62.

Row 81: Ch 3, sc in ch-2 sp from previous row, change to cranberry on last yo and pull through, [ch 2, 3 dc in same ch-2 sp, sc in next ch-2 sp from previous row] across, turn.

Rows 82–90: Rep row 62.

Rows 91–118: Rep rows 61–88.

Row 119: Ch 3, sc in ch-2 sp from previous row, ch 2, 3 dc in same ch-2 sp, sc in last ch-2 sp from previous row, ch 3 and turn, sl st in ch-2 sp from previous row. Fasten off.

Crocodile Stitch Border

Make 2.

Row 1: With sorbet, ch 151, dc in back bar of 4th ch from hook, ch 1, sk 1 ch, dc in back bar of next ch, [ch 1, sk 1 ch, dc in back bar of each of next 2 chs, ch 1, sk 1 ch, dc in back bar of next ch] 29 times, turn. *(90 dc, 59 ch sps)*

Row 2: Ch 1, sc in first dc, turn, with RS facing, rotate piece to work around post of first dc, 5 dc around first dc, **picot** *(see Special Stitches)*. Now working **scales** *(see Pattern Notes)*, rotate piece 180 degrees, 5 dc around next dc, [turn, with WS facing, sc in next dc, turn, with RS facing, rotate piece, 5 dc around next dc, picot, rotate piece 180 degrees, 5 dc around next dc] across, turn. *(30 scales)*

Row 3: Ch 3, sc in sp at center of first scale, ch 4 *(counts as dc, ch-1)*, [dc in dc from 2 rows below beside sc already worked, sk sc, dc in same dc on other side of sk sc, ch 1, dc in sp at center of next scale, ch 1] across, end with 2 dc in last sc.

Row 4: Ch 3 and rotate work with RS facing, 5 dc around post of first dc, sc in first sc from 2 rows below, 5 dc around post of next dc, [turn, with WS facing, sc in top of next dc, turn, 5 dc around post of next dc, sc in sc between scales from 2 rows below, 5 dc around post of next dc] across, end with sc in 3rd ch of beg ch-4, turn.

Row 5: Ch 3, dc in sc at base of ch, dc in sp at center of next scale, [ch 1, dc in dc from 2 rows below beside sc already worked, sk sc, dc in same dc on other side of sk sc, ch 1, dc in sp at center of next scale] across, turn.

Row 6: Ch 1, sc in first dc, turn, with RS facing, [5 dc around post of next dc**, sc in downward-facing sc between scales, 5 dc along post of next dc, turn, sc in next dc, turn] across, ending last rep at **, sc in last sc from 2 rows below, 5 dc along post of next dc, turn.

Rows 7 & 8: Rep rows 3 and 4, change to coulis in last st.

Rows 9–16: With coulis, [work rows 5 and 6, work rows 3 and 4] twice. At end of row 16, change to cranberry in last st.

Rows 17–24: With cranberry, [work rows 5 and 6, work rows 3 and 4] twice.

Row 25: Ch 1, [2 sc in ch-1 sp from 2 rows below, sc in center of scale, 2 sc in ch-1 sp from 2 rows below, sc in dc from 2 rows below next to sc already worked] across. Fasten off. *(180 sc)*

Finishing

Lay short edge of Center Block adjacent to sc edge of one Border with RS up, **whipstitch edges through back lps** *(see illustration)* to seam. Rep on other short edge of Center Block. Weave in all ends. ●

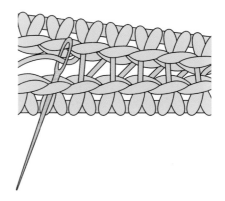

Whipstitch Edges Through Back Loops

Water Lily Throw

Skill Level

■■■■ EXPERIENCED

Finished Measurement

40 inches square

Materials

- Berroco Comfort DK light (DK) weight acrylic/nylon yarn (1¾ oz/178 yds/50g per skein):
    - 7 skeins #2726 cornflower
    - 6 skeins #2740 seedling
    - 5 skeins #2702 pearl
    - 2 skeins #2719 sunshine
- Size G/6/4mm crochet hook or size needed to obtain gauge
- Stitch markers
- Tapestry needle

Gauge

19 dc = 4 inches; 10 dc rnds = 4 inches; each Block measures 9½ inches

Pattern Notes

Some rounds are crocheted after turning the work; take note of the right-side and wrong-side designations.

Place marker in the first stitch of first round and move it to the first stitch of next 6 consecutive rounds as they are worked.

Join with slip stitch as indicated unless otherwise stated.

Chain-3 at beginning of round counts as first double crochet unless otherwise stated.

Special Stitches

Sideways slip stitch (sslst): Insert hook under front lp of indicated st and immediately under front vertical lp of same st *(see illustration)*, yo, draw through all lps on hook.

Front Loop & Side

Sideways single crochet (ssc): Insert hook under front lp of st just made and immediately under front vertical lp of same st *(see above illustration)*, yo, pull up lp, yo, draw through both lps on hook.

Pinned picot: Ch 2, insert hook under front lp of indicated st and under 2 strands of corresponding st in cornflower fabric when petal or leaf is laid flat, yo and pull through all strands on hook, yo and pull through 2 lps on hook.

Slip stitch join (sl st join): Place 2 Blocks with RS facing each other, working through both layers, join cornflower in corner ch-2 sp, [insert hook under **front lp** *(see Stitch Guide)* of next st in near Block and back lp of next st in far Block, yo and pull through all lps on hook] across to join. Fasten off.

Picot: Ch 2, **ssc** *(see Special Stitches)* in side of st at base of ch-2.

Throw

Block
Make 16.

Rnd 1: With sunshine make **slip ring** (see illustration), ch 1 (does not count as st), [sc, tr] 6 times into ring, tighten ring, **join** (see Pattern Notes) in beg sc. (6 sc, 6 tr)

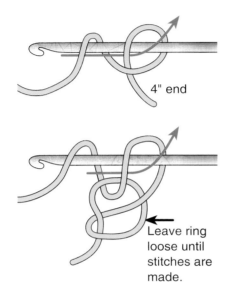

4" end

Leave ring loose until stitches are made.

Slip Ring

Rnd 2: Ch 1, (sc, tr) in join, (sc, tr) in each of next 11 sts, join in first sc. (12 sc, 12 tr)

Rnd 3: Ch 1, (sc, tr, sc) in same st, [sk next tr, (sc, tr, sc) in next sc] 11 times, join in first sc. (12 tr, 24 sc)

Rnd 4: Ch 1, sc in join, [sk tr, (sc, tr) in next sc, sc in next sc] 11 times, sk next tr, (sc, tr) in next sc, join in first sc. Fasten off. (12 tr, 24 sc)

Note: The tr sts will naturally pop out on the WS of the fabric. For the purposes of this pattern, the "bumpy" side will be considered the RS of the fabric.

Rnd 5 (RS): Turn so tr st bumps are facing, with pearl, join with hdc in sc following any tr, hdc in same st, 2 hdc in next sc, [ch 5, **sslst** (see Special Stitches) in hdc at base of ch, sk tr, 2 hdc in each of next 2 sc] 11 times, ch 5, sslst in hdc at base of ch, sk tr, join in first hdc. (12 ch-5 arches and 48 hdc)

Rnd 6: Ch 3 (see Pattern Notes), dc in next hdc, ch 6, sslst in dc at base of ch, dc in next hdc, ch 2, [sk next ch-5 arch, dc in each of next 2 hdc, ch 6, sslst in dc at base of ch, dc in next hdc, ch 2] 11 times, join in top of beg ch-3. Fasten off. (12 ch-6 arches, 12 ch-2 sps, 36 dc)

Rnd 7: With seedling, join with tr in any ch-2 sp, ch 2, [sk next ch-6 arch, (3 tr, ch 6, sslst in tr at base of ch, 2 tr) in next ch-2 sp, ch 2] 11 times, (3 tr, ch 6, sslst in tr at base of ch, tr) in next ch-2 sp, join in first tr. (12 ch-6 arches, 12 ch-2 sps, 60 tr) Place marker in any ch-2 sp.

Rnd 8: Sl st in next ch-2 sp, ch 1, 2 sc in same ch-2 sp, [sc in each of next 2 tr, sk next tr, ch 2, reach behind ch-6 arch and hdc in each of next 2 tr, 3 dc in next ch-2 sp, tr in next tr, 2 tr in next tr, sk next tr, ch 3, reach behind ch-6 arch and 2 tr in next tr, tr in next tr, 3 dc in next ch-2 sp, hdc in each of next 2 tr, sk next tr, ch 2, reach behind ch-6 arch and sc in each of next 2 tr**, 2 sc in next ch-2 sp] 4 times, ending last rep at **, join in first sc. Fasten off. (104 sts, 4 ch-3 corners)

Rnd 9: With cornflower, join with sc in any ch-3 corner sp, (ch 2, 2 sc) in same sp, sc in each of next 8 sts, 2 sc in ch-2 sp behind arch, sc in each of next 6 sts, 2 sc in ch-2 sp behind arch, sc in each of next 8 sts, [(2 sc, ch 2, 2 sc) in ch-3 corner sp, sc in each of next 8 sts, 2 sc in ch-2 sp behind arch, sc in each of next 6 sts, 2 sc in ch-2 sp behind arch, sc in each of next 8 sts] 3 times, sc in next ch-3 sp, join in first sc. (120 sc, 4 ch-2 corners)

Rnd 10: Sl st in ch-2 corner sp, (ch 6, dc) in same sp, [dc in each of next 30 sc, (dc, ch 3, dc) in ch-2 corner sp] 3 times, dc in each of next 30 sc, join in 3rd ch of beg ch-6. (128 dc, 4 ch-3 corners)

Rnd 11: Sl st in ch-3 sp, ch 1, (sc, ch 3, sc) in same sp, *[(sc, hdc, dc, 2 tr, dc, hdc, sc) in **back lps** (see Stitch Guide) across next 8 sts] 4 times, (sc, ch 3, sc) in next ch-3 corner sp, rep from * twice, [(sc, hdc, dc, 2 tr, dc, hdc, sc) in back lps across next 8 sts] 4 times, join in first sc. (136 sts, 4 ch-3 corners)

Rnd 12: Sl st in ch-3 sp, ch 4, (tr, ch 2, 2 tr) in same sp, *[(2 tr, dc, hdc, 2 sc, hdc, dc) in back lps across next 8 sts] 4 times, tr in back lp of each of next 2 sts, (2 tr, ch 2, 2 tr) in next ch-3 sp*, rep from * twice, [(2 tr, dc, hdc, 2 sc, hdc, dc) in back lps across next 8 sts] 4 times, tr in back lp of each of next 2 sts, join in top of beg ch-4. *(152 sts, 4 ch-2 corners)*

Rnd 13: Sl st in next tr, sl st in ch-3 sp, ch 3, (dc, ch 2, 2 dc) in same sp, [dc in back lp of each of next 38 sts, (2 dc, ch 2, 2 dc) in ch-2 corner sp] 3 times, dc in back lp of each of next 38 sts, join in top of beg ch. Fasten off. *(168 dc, 4 ch-2 corners)*

Surface Crochet

Outer Petals
Rnd 14: Join seedling with sc to marked ch-2 sp from rnd 7, [(6 tr, **pinned picot**—*see Special Stitches*, 6 tr) in next ch-6 arch, sc in next ch-2 from rnd 7 between sts] 11 times, (6 tr, pinned picot, 6 tr) in next ch-6 arch, join in first sc. Fasten off. *(12 crocodile leaves, 12 sc)*

Middle Petals
Rnd 15: Join pearl with sc in ch-2 sp from rnd 6 between any 2 dc, [(dc, 5 tr, pinned picot, 5 tr, dc) in next ch-6 arch, sc in next ch-2 sp between 2 dc] 11 times, (dc, 5 tr, pinned picot, 5 tr, dc) in next ch-6 arch, join in first sc. Fasten off. *(12 crocodile petals, 12 sc)*

Inner Petals
Rnd 16: Join pearl with sc in center hdc from rnd 5 between ch-5 arches beside dc already there, [(hdc, 2 dc, 2 tr, pinned picot, 2 tr, 2 dc, hdc) in next ch-5 arch, sk 1 rnd 5 hdc, sc in next hdc beside dc already there] 11 times, (hdc, 2 dc, 2 tr, pinned picot, 2 tr, 2 dc, hdc) in next ch-5 arch, join in first sc. Fasten off. *(12 crocodile petals, 12 sc)*

Weave in ends.

Assembly

Strip
Make 4.

Work **sl st join** *(see Special Stitches)* to join 4 Blocks to each other to form Strip.

Throw
Work sl st join to connect 4 Strips to form a square.

Edging
Rnd 1: With cornflower, join with dc in any ch-2 corner sp, (dc, ch 3, 2 dc) in same sp, *[dc in back lp of each of next 42 sts, tr in next ch-2 sp, 2 tr in sl st join between Blocks, tr in ch-2 sp] 3 times, dc in back lp of each of next 42 sts, (2 dc, ch 3, 2 dc) in ch-2 corner sp, rep from * twice, [dc in back lp of each of next 42 sts, tr in next ch-2 sp, 2 tr in sl st join between Blocks, tr in ch-2 sp] 3 times, dc in back lp of each of next 42 sts, join in first dc. Fasten off. *(736 dc, 4 ch-3 corner sps)*

Rnd 2: Join seedling with sc in any ch-3 corner sp, (ch 3, tr, ch 3, tr, ch 3, sc) in same sp, *ch 2, sk 2 sts, [sc in next st, (ch 3, tr, ch 3, tr, ch 3) in next st, sc in next st, ch 7, sk 5 sts] 22 times, sc in next st, (ch 3, tr, ch 3, tr, ch 3) in next st, sc in next st, ch 2, sk 3 sts, (sc, ch 3, tr, ch 3, tr, ch 3, sc) in ch-3 corner sp, rep from * twice, ch 2, sk 2 sts, [sc in next st, (ch 3, tr, ch 3, tr, ch 3) in next st, sc in next st, ch 7, sk 5 sts] 22 times, sc in next st, (ch 3, tr, ch 3, tr, ch 3) in next st, sc in next st, ch 2, sk 3 sts, join in first sc. *(23 fans on each side and 1 fan in each corner)*

Rnd 3: Ch 1, *4 hdc in next ch-3 sp, (2 hdc, **picot** *(see Special Stitches)*, 2 hdc) in next ch-3 sp, 4 hdc in next ch-3 sp, sc in ch-2 sp, [4 hdc in next ch-3 sp, (2 hdc, picot, 2 hdc) in next ch-3 sp, 4 hdc in next ch-3 sp, sk 3 ch, sc in next ch] 22 times, 4 hdc in next ch-3 sp, (2 hdc, picot, 2 hdc) in next ch-3 sp, 4 hdc in next ch-3 sp, sc in ch-2 sp, rep from * 3 times, join in first hdc. Fasten off.

Finishing
Weave in all ends. ●

Westphalia Afghan

Skill Level

 INTERMEDIATE

Finished Measurements

48 inches wide × 60 inches long

Materials

- Berroco Comfort medium (worsted) weight acrylic/nylon yarn (3½ oz/210 yds/ 100g per skein):
  - 12 skeins #9701 ivory
  - 1 skein #9760 beet root
- Size I/9/5.5mm crochet hook or size needed to obtain gauge
- Tapestry needle

Gauge

In mesh pattern: 16 sts = 4 inches; 9 rows = 4 inches

Pattern Notes

Chain-3 at beginning of row counts as first double crochet unless otherwise stated.

Join with slip stitch as indicated unless otherwise stated.

Special Stitches

Mesh: *Dc in next dc, ch 1, sk 1 st, rep from * indicated number of reps.

Sideways single crochet (ssc): Insert hook under front lp of dc just made and immediately under front vertical lp of same dc *(see illustration)*, yo, pull up lp, yo, draw through both lps on hook.

Front Loop & Side

Picot: Ch 2, **ssc** *(see Special Stitches)* in side of st at base of ch-2.

Tack: Yo, insert hook through picot at top of crocodile scale and through next sc, yo and pull through both sts, [yo, pull through 2 lps] twice.

Sideways slip stitch (sslst): Insert hook under front lp of sc just made, and immediately under front vertical lp of same sc *(see above illustration)*, yo, draw through all lps on hook.

Fan: ([Tr, ch 1] 6 times, tr) in indicated sp.

Afghan

Row 1 (RS): With ivory, ch 174, dc **in back bar** *(see illustration)* of 4th ch from hook, dc in each ch across, turn. *(171 dc)*

Back Bar of Chain

Row 2: Ch 3 *(see Pattern Notes)*, dc in next dc, 83 **mesh** *(see Special Stitches)*, dc in each of last 3 dc, turn. *(83 ch sps, 88 dc)*

Row 3: Ch 3, dc in next dc, 6 mesh, [sk 1 dc, 3 dc in next ch sp, ch 1, sk next ch sp, 8 mesh] 7 times, sk 1 dc, 3 dc in next ch sp, ch 1, sk next ch sp, 5 mesh, dc in each of next 3 sts, turn.

Row 4: Ch 3, dc in next dc, 5 mesh, [sk 1 dc, 3 dc in next ch sp, ch 6, **ssc** *(see Special Stitches)*, 3 dc in next ch sp, ch 1, sk 1 ch sp, 6 mesh] 7 times, sk 1 dc, 3 dc in next ch sp, ch 6, ssc, 3 dc in next ch sp, ch 1, sk 1 ch sp, 4 mesh, dc in each of next 3 sts, turn.

Row 5: Ch 3, dc in next dc, 4 mesh, [sk 1 dc, (dc, hdc, sc) in next ch sp, (6 dc, **picot** *(see Special Stitches)*, 6 dc) in ch-6 sp, (sc, hdc, dc) in next ch sp, ch 1, sk next ch sp, 4 mesh] 7 times, sk 1 dc, (dc, hdc, sc) in next ch sp, (6 dc, picot, 6 dc) in ch-6 sp, (sc, hdc, dc) in next ch sp, ch 1, sk next ch sp, 3 mesh, dc in each of next 3 sts, turn. *(8 crocodile scales)*

Row 6: Ch 3, dc in next dc, 3 mesh, [sk 1 dc, 3 dc in next ch sp, ch 5, fold top of crocodile scale to RS and sc in ch-6 sp from previous row (between dc below picot), ch 5, 3 dc in next ch sp, ch 1, sk next ch sp, 2 mesh] 8 times, dc in each of next 3 sts, turn.

Row 7: Ch 3, dc in next dc, 2 mesh, [sk 1 dc, 3 dc in next ch sp, ch 3, 2 sc in ch-5 sp, sc in sc, 2 sc in ch-5 sp, ch 3, 3 dc in next ch sp, ch 1, sk 1 dc] 8 times, 1 mesh, dc in each of next 3 sts, turn.

Row 8: Ch 3, dc in next dc, 3 mesh, [3 dc in next ch sp, ch 3, sk 1 sc, sc in each of next 3 sc, ch 3, 3 dc in next ch sp, ch 1, sk 2 dc, 2 mesh] 8 times, dc in each of next 3 sts, turn.

Row 9: Ch 3, dc in next dc, 4 mesh, [3 dc in next ch sp, ch 2, sk 1 sc, **tack** *(see Special Stitches)*, ch 2, 3 dc in next ch sp, ch 1, sk 2 dc, 4 mesh] 7 times, 3 dc in next ch-3 sp, ch 2, sk 1 sc, tack, ch 2, 3 dc in next ch-3 sp, ch 1, sk 2 dc, 3 mesh, dc in each of next 3 sts, turn.

Row 10: Ch 3, dc in next dc, 5 mesh, [3 dc in next ch sp, ch 1, 3 dc in next ch sp, ch 1, sk 2 dc, 6 mesh] 7 times, 3 dc in next ch sp, ch 1, 3 dc in next ch sp, ch 1, sk 2 dc, 4 mesh, dc in each of next 3 sts, turn.

Row 11: Ch 3, dc in next dc, 6 mesh, [3 dc in next ch sp, ch 1, sk 2 dc, 8 mesh] 7 times, 3 dc in next ch sp, ch 1, sk 2 dc, 5 mesh, dc in each of next 3 sts, turn.

Row 12: Ch 3, dc in next dc, 83 mesh, dc in each of next 3 sts, turn. *(88 dc, 83 ch)*

Row 13: Ch 3, dc in each of next 170 sts, turn.

Row 14: Ch 3, dc in next dc, 12 mesh, dc in next dc, ch 2, sk 2 dc, [sc in each of next 4 sts, ch 6, sk 6 sts] 11 times, sc in each of next 4 sts, ch 2, sk 1 st, 12 mesh, dc in each of next 3 sts, turn.

Row 15: Ch 3, dc in next dc, 6 mesh, sk 1 dc, 3 dc in next ch sp, ch 1, sk next ch sp, 4 mesh, dc in next dc, 2 dc in ch-2 sp, [dc in each of next 4 sc, 8 dc in next ch sp] 11 times, dc in each of next 4 sc, 2 dc in ch-2 sp, 5 mesh, sk 1 dc, 3 dc in next ch sp, ch 1, sk next ch sp, 5 mesh, dc in each of next 3 sts, turn.

Row 16: Ch 3, dc in next dc, 5 mesh, sk 1 dc, 3 dc in next ch sp, ch 6, ssc, 3 dc in next ch sp, ch 1, sk 1 ch sp, 3 mesh, dc in next dc, [ch 6, sk 8 dc, sc in each of next 4 sts] 11 times, ch 6, sk 8 dc, 4 mesh, sk 1 dc, 3 dc in next ch sp, ch 6, ssc, 3 dc in next ch sp, ch 1, sk 1 ch sp, 4 mesh, dc in each of next 3 sts, turn.

Row 17: Ch 3, dc in next dc, 4 mesh, sk 1 dc, (dc, hdc, sc) in next ch sp, (6 dc, picot, 6 dc) in ch-6 sp, (sc, hdc, dc) in next ch sp, ch 1, sk next ch sp, 2 mesh, dc in next dc, [8 dc in ch-6 sp, dc in each of next 4 sc] 11 times, 8 dc in ch-6 sp, 3 mesh, sk 1 dc, (dc, hdc, sc) in next ch sp, (6 dc, picot, 6 dc) in ch-6 sp, (sc, hdc, dc) in next ch sp, ch 1, sk next ch sp, 3 mesh, dc in each of next 3 sts, turn.

Row 18: Ch 3, dc in next dc, 3 mesh, sk 1 dc, 3 dc in next ch sp, ch 5, fold top of crocodile scale to RS and sc in ch-6 sp, ch 5, 3 dc in next ch sp, ch 1, sk next ch sp, 1 mesh, dc in next dc, ch 2, sk 2 dc, [sc in each of next 4 dc, ch 6, sk 8 dc] 11 times, sc in each of next 4 dc, ch 2, sk 2 dc, 2 mesh, sk 1 dc, 3 dc in next ch sp, ch 5, fold top of crocodile scale to RS and sc in ch-6 sp, ch 5, 3 dc in next ch sp, ch 1, sk next ch sp, 2 mesh, dc in each of next 3 sts, turn.

Row 19: Ch 3, dc in next dc, 2 mesh, sk 1 dc, 3 dc in next ch sp, ch 3, 2 sc in ch-5 sp, sc in sc, 2 sc in next ch-5 sp, ch 3, 3 dc in next ch sp, ch 1, sk 1 ch sp, dc in next dc, 2 dc in ch-2 sp, [dc in each of next 4 sc, 8 dc in next ch sp] 11 times, dc in each of next 4 sc, 2 dc in ch-2 sp, 1 mesh, sk 1 ch sp, 3 dc in next ch sp, ch 3, 2 sc in ch-5 sp, sc in sc, 2 sc in ch-5 sp, ch 3, 3 dc in next ch sp, ch 1, sk 1 dc, 1 mesh, dc in each of next 3 sts, turn.

Row 20: Ch 3, dc in next dc, 3 mesh, 3 dc in next ch sp, ch 3, sk 1 sc, sc in each of next 3 sc, ch 3, 3 dc in next ch sp, ch 1, sk 2 dc, 1 mesh, dc in next dc, [ch 6, sk 8 dc, sc in each of next 4 dc] 11 times, ch 6, sk 8 dc, 2 mesh, 3 dc in next ch sp, ch 3, sk 1 sc, sc in each of next 3 sc, ch 3, 3 dc in next ch sp, ch 1, sk 2 dc, 2 mesh, dc in each of next 3 sts, turn.

Row 21: Ch 3, dc in next dc, 4 mesh, 3 dc in next ch sp, ch 2, sk 1 sc, tack, ch 2, 3 dc in next ch sp, ch 1, sk 2 dc, 2 mesh, dc in dc, [8 dc in ch-6 sp, dc in each of next 4 sc] 11 times, 8 dc in ch-6, 3 mesh, 3 dc in next ch-3 sp, ch 2, sk 1 sc, tack, ch 2, 3 dc in next ch-3 sp, ch 1, sk 2 dc, 3 mesh, dc in each of next 3 sts, turn.

Row 22: Ch 3, dc in next dc, 5 mesh, 3 dc in next ch sp, ch 1, 3 dc in next ch sp, ch 1, sk 2 dc, 3 mesh, dc in next dc, ch 2, sk 2 dc, [sc in each of next 4 sts, ch 6, sk 8 dc] 11 times, sc in each of next 4 sts, ch 2, sk 2 dc, 4 mesh, 3 dc in next ch sp, ch 1, 3 dc in next ch sp, ch 1, sk 2 dc, 4 mesh, dc in each of next 3 sts, turn.

Row 23: Ch 3, dc in next dc, 6 mesh, 3 dc in next ch sp, ch 1, sk 2 dc, 4 mesh, dc in next dc, 2 dc in ch-2 sp, [dc in each of next 4 sc, 8 dc in next ch sp] 11 times, dc in each of next 4 sc, 2 dc in ch-2 sp, 5 mesh, 3 dc in next ch sp, ch 1, sk 2 dc, 5 mesh, dc in each of next 3 sts, turn.

Row 24: Ch 3, dc in next dc, 12 mesh, dc in next dc, [ch 6, sk 8 dc, sc in each of next 4 dc] 11 times, ch 6, sk 8 dc, 12 mesh, dc in each of next 3 sts, turn.

Row 25: Ch 3, dc in each of next 26 sts, [8 dc in ch-6 sp, dc in each of next 4 sc] 11 times, 8 dc in ch-6, dc across, turn.

Row 26: Ch 3, dc in next dc, 12 mesh, dc in next dc, ch 2, sk 2 dc, [sc in each of next 4 sts, ch 6, sk 8 dc] 11 times, sc in each of next 4 sts, ch 2, sk 2 dc, 12 mesh, dc in each of next 3 sts, turn.

Rows 27–98: [Rep rows 15–26 consecutively] 6 times.

Rows 99–108: [Rep rows 15–24 consecutively] once.

Row 109: Ch 3, dc in each of next 26 sts, [6 dc in ch-6 sp, dc in each of next 4 sc] 11 times, 7 dc in ch-6 sp, dc across, turn.

Rows 110–121: [Rep rows 2–13 consecutively] once. Do not fasten off.

Edging

Rnd 1: Now working in rnds, working along long side, ch 1, *[10 sc, ch 6, **ssslst** *(see Special Stitches)*] 23 times evenly across (by working 2 sc in each row end), work 9 sc evenly across ends of last 6 rows, place marker in first ch-6 sp made, sc in corner, ch 6, ssslst, rotate work to continue across short side, [sc in each of next 10 sts, ch 6, ssslst] 16 times, sc in each of next 10 sts, ch 6, ssslst, rep from * once, **join** *(see Pattern Notes)* in first sc.

Rnd 2: Ch 6, *sk 3 sc, dc in next st, ch 3, dc in next st, ch 3, sk 3 sc, dc in next sc, [ch 1, sk ch-6 sp, dc in next sc, ch 3, sk 3 sc, dc in next sc, ch 3, dc in next sc, ch 3, sk 3 sc, dc in next sc] 23 times, ch 3, rotate work, sk ch-6 sp, dc in next sc, ch 3, sk 3 sc, dc in next sc, ch 3, dc in next sc, ch 3, sk 3 sc, dc in next sc, [ch 1, sk ch-6 sp, dc in next sc, ch 3, sk 3 sc, dc in next sc, ch 3, dc in next sc, ch 3**, sk 3 sc, dc in next sc] 16 times, ch 3, rotate work, sk ch-6 sp, rep from * once, ending at **, sk sp, sl st in 3rd st of beg ch-6.

Rnd 3: Sl st in next ch, ch 1, sc in same ch-3 sp, * [**fan** *(see Special Stitches)* in next ch-3 sp, sk next ch-3 sp, sc in next dc, sc in ch-1 sp, sc in next dc, sk next ch-3 sp] 23 times, fan in next ch-3 sp, sc in next ch-3 sp, fan in corner ch-3 sp, sc in next ch-3 sp, rotate work, [fan in next ch-3 sp, sk next ch-3 sp, sc in next dc, sc in ch-1 sp, sc in dc, sk next ch-3 sp] 16 times, fan in next ch-3 sp, sc in next ch-3 sp, fan in corner ch-3 sp**, sc in next ch-3 sp, rotate work, rep from * once, ending at **, sl st in beg ch-1 to join.

Rnd 4: Sl st in next tr, sl st in ch sp, ch 1, sc in same sp, ch 2, (dc, ch 2) in each of next 4 ch-1 sps, dc in next ch-1 sp, ch 1, sk next sc, sc in next sc, ch 1, [(dc, ch 2) in each of next 5 ch-1 sps, dc in next ch-1 sp, ch 1, sk next sc, sc in next sc, ch 1] 22 times, (dc, ch 2) in each of next 5 ch-1 sps, sc in next ch-1 sp, sc in next ch-1 sp, ch 2, (dc, ch 2) in each of next 4 ch-1 sps, *rotate work, sc in next ch-1 sp, (sc, ch 2) in next ch-1 sp, (dc, ch 2) in each of next 4 ch-1 sps, (dc, ch 1) in next ch-1 sp, sk next sc, (sc, ch 1) in next sc, [(dc, ch 2) in each of next 5 ch-1 sps, (dc, ch 1) in next ch-1 sp, sk next sc, sc in next sc, ch 1] 15 times, (dc, ch 2) in each of next 5 ch-1 sps, sc in next ch-1 sp, sc in next ch-1 sp, ch 2, (dc, ch 2) in each of next 4 ch-1 sps*, rotate work, sc in next ch-1 sp, sc in next ch-1 sp, ch 2, (dc, ch 2) in each of next 4 ch-1 sps, dc in next ch-1 sp, ch 1, sk next sc, sc in next sc, ch 1, [(dc, ch 2) in each of next 5 ch-1 sps, dc in next ch-1 sp, ch 1, sk next sc, sc in next sc, ch 1] 23 times, (dc, ch 2) in each of next 5 ch-1 sps, sc in next ch-1 sp, sc in next ch-1 sp, ch 2, (dc, ch 2) in each of next 4 ch-1 sps, rep between *, sc in next ch-2 sp, join in first sc.

Rnd 5: Sl st in next ch-2 sp, ch 1, (sc, ch 3, sc) in same sp, (sc, ch 3, sc) in each of next 4 ch-2 sps, *[sc in next ch-1 sp, ch 3, sc in next ch-1 sp, (sc, ch 3, sc) in each of next 5 ch-2 sps] 23 times, [(sc, ch 3, sc) in each of next 5 ch-2 sps] 2 times, [sc in next ch-1 sp, ch 3, sc in next ch-1 sp, (sc, ch 3, sc) in each of next 5 ch-2 sps] 16 times**, [(sc, ch 3, sc) in each of next 5 ch-2 sps] 2 times, rep from * once ending at **, (sc, ch 3, sc) in each of next 5 ch-2 sp, join in first sc.

Fasten off.

Rnd 6: Join beet root with tr in marked ch-6 sp, 5 dc in same ch sp, sc in sc between fans from rnd 4, (5 dc, tr) in same ch-6 sp, sk 2 sc from rnd 1, sc in next sc from rnd 1, (hdc, dc, hdc) in sc between next 2 dc from rnd 2, sc in next sc from rnd 1, *[(1 tr, 5 dc) in next ch-6 sp, sc in sc between fans from rnd 4, (5 dc, 1 tr) in same ch-6 sp, sk 2 sc from rnd 1, sc in next sc from rnd 1, (hdc, dc, hdc) in sc between next 2 dc from rnd 2, sc in next sc from rnd 1] 22 times, (2 tr, 5 dc) in corner ch-6 sp, sc in center tr of corner fan from rnd 3, (5 dc, 2 tr) in same ch-6 sp, sk 2 sc from rnd 1, sc in next sc from rnd 1, (hdc, dc, hdc) in sc between next 2 dc from rnd 2, sc in next sc from rnd 1, rotate work, [(1 tr, 5 dc) in next ch-6 sp, sc in sc between fans from rnd 4, (5 dc, 1 tr) in same ch-6 sp, sk 2 sc, sc in next sc from rnd 1, (hdc, dc, hdc) in sc between next 2 dc from rnd 2, sc in next sc from rnd 1] 16 times, (2 tr, 5 dc) in corner ch-6 sp, sc in center tr of corner fan from rnd 3, (5 dc, 2 tr) in same ch-6 sp, sk 2 sc, sc in next sc, (hdc, dc, hdc) in sc between next 2 dc from rnd 2, sc in next sc from rnd 1**, rotate work, (1 tr, 5 dc) in next ch-6 sp, sc in sc between fans, (5 dc, 1 tr) in same ch-6 sp, sk 2 sc, sc in next sc from rnd 1, (hdc, dc, hdc) in sc between next 2 dc from rnd 2, sc in next sc from rnd 1, rep from * once, end at **, join in first tr.

Fasten off.

Finishing
Weave in ends. ●

Dragonslayer Afghan

Skill Level

 INTERMEDIATE

Finished Measurements

48 inches wide × 64 inches long

Materials

- Berroco Comfort medium (worsted) weight acrylic/nylon yarn (3½ oz/210 yds/100g per skein):
  - 6 skeins each #9720 hummus and #9785 falseberry heather
  - 5 skeins #9795 blueberry heather
- Size J/10/6mm crochet hook or size needed to obtain gauge
- Stitch markers
- Tapestry needle

Gauge

12 dc = 4 inches; 7 dc rows = 4 inches

Pattern Notes

Treble crochets and front post treble crochets at end of rows count as chain-4 spaces.

Join with slip stitch as indicated unless otherwise stated.

Special Stitches

Sideways single crochet (ssc): Insert hook under front lp of st just made and immediately under front vertical lp of same st *(see illustration)*, yo, pull up lp, yo, draw through both lps on hook.

Front Loop & Side

Picot: Ch 2, **ssc** *(see Special Stitches)* in side of st at base of ch-2.

Slip stitch in front and back loops (sl st in front and back lps): Yo, insert hook under **front lp** *(see Stitch Guide)* of st in near Panel and then in **back lp** *(see Stitch Guide)* of st in far Panel, yo and pull through all lps on hook.

Afghan

Panel

Make 6.

Scales Strip

Row 1: With hummus, ch 9, dc in 6th st from hook *(counts as ch-1, dc, ch-1)*, place marker in sp just made, dc in next st, ch 1, sk 1 st, dc in last st.

Row 2: Ch 1, rotate work 90 degrees, (5 dc, **picot**— *see Special Stitches*) around post of 2nd dc from hook, rotate work 180 degrees, 5 dc around post of next dc *(scale made)*, ch 1, **fpsc** *(see Stitch Guide)* around post of marked ch-5, leave marker in place.

Row 3: Ch 4, 2 dc in sp at center of previous scale, ch 1, **fptr** *(see Stitch Guide and Pattern Notes)* around post of next dc.

Row 4: Ch 1, rotate work 90 degrees, (5 dc, picot) around post of last dc made, rotate work 180 degrees, 5 dc around post of next dc, ch 1, fpsc around ch-4.

Row 5: Ch 4, 2 dc in sp at center of previous scale, ch 1, fptr around post of last tr.

Row 6: Ch 1, rotate work 90 degrees, (5 dc, picot) around post of last dc made, rotate work 180 degrees, 5 dc around post of next dc, ch 1, fpsc around ch-4.

[Rep rows 5 and 6] 69 times, ch 3, **join** *(see Pattern Notes)* around post of tr. Fasten off. *(72 scales)*

Mile-a-Minute Motif
Row 1: With RS facing and with blueberry, join with dc in marked sp, 2 dc in same sp, 3 dc in each of next 71 ch-4 sps, ch 1, 6 dc in ch-3 sp, ch 1, 3 dc in each of next 71 tr-sp, ch 1, 3 dc in each of next 2 ch sps, ch 1, join in first dc. *(444 dc, 4 ch sps)*

Row 2: Ch 2 *(counts as first sc)*, hdc in each of next 2 dc, dc in each of next 2 dc, tr in each of next 2 dc, dc in each of next 2 dc, hdc in each of next 2 dc, sc in next dc, *sc in next dc, hdc in each of next 2 dc, dc in each of next 2 dc, tr in each of next 2 dc, dc in each of next 2 dc, hdc in each of next 2 dc, sc in next dc*, rep between * across to 6 dc at end, ch 1, (sc, hdc) in next dc, (hdc, dc) in next dc, (dc, tr) in next dc, ch 1, (tr, dc) in next dc, (dc, hdc) in next dc, (hdc, sc) in next dc, ch 1, rep between * across to 6 dc st end, ch 1, (sc, hdc) in next dc, (hdc, dc) in next dc, (dc, tr) in next dc, ch 1, (tr, dc) in next dc, (dc, hdc) in next dc, (hdc, sc) in next dc, ch 1, join in ch-2 sp. *(456 sts, 4 ch sps)*

Row 3: Ch 2, sc in **back lp** *(see Stitch Guide)* of each of next 222 sts, 3 sc in ch-1 sp, sc in back lp of each of next 230 sts, 3 sc in ch-1 sp, sc in back lp of each of next 7 sts, join in ch-2 sp. Fasten off. *(466 sc)*

Row 4: With falseberry, join with dc in a sc at one tip of Panel, dc in same st, dc in each of next 7 sts, 3 dc in next st, *tr in next sc, dc in each of next 2 sc, hdc in each of next 2 sc, sc in each of next 2 sc, hdc in each of next 2 sc, dc in each of next 2 sc, tr in next sc*, rep between * 17 times, [3 dc in next sc, dc in each of next 7 sc] twice, 3 dc in next st, rep between * 18 times, 3 dc in next sc, dc in each of next 7 sc, 1 dc in first sc, join in first dc. *(478 sts)*

Row 5: Ch 3, dc in same st, dc in each of next 10 sts, 3 dc in next st, dc in each of next 216 sts, [3 dc in next dc, dc in each of next 10 sts] twice, 3 dc in next dc, dc in each of next 216 sts, 3 dc in next dc, dc in each of next 10 sts, dc in same st as beg ch-3, join in top of ch-3. *(490 dc)*

Row 6: Ch 2, sc in back lp of each st around, join in ch-2, turn. *(490 sc)*

Row 7 (WS): Ch 1, (sc, tr, sc) in same st, [tr in next st, sc in next st] 7 times, (tr, sc) in next st, [tr in next st, sc in next st] 114 times, tr in next st, (sc, tr, sc) in next st, [tr in next st, sc in next st] 7 times, (tr, sc) in next st, [tr in next st, sc in next st] 114 times, tr in next st, join in first sc. Fasten off. *(496 sts)*

Row 8: With RS facing and with hummus, join with sc in tr at tip of other end of Panel, sc in same st, sc in each of next 15 sts, 3 sc in next tr, place marker in last sc of 3-sc group just made, sc in each of next 215 sts, 3 sc in next tr, place marker in first sc of 3-sc group just made, [sc in each of next 15 sts, 3 sc in next tr] twice, place marker in last sc of 3-sc group just made, sc in each of next 215, 3 sc in next tr, place marker in first sc of 3-sc group just made, sc in each of next 15 sts, sc in first st, join in first sc. Fasten off. *(508 sc)*

Assembly
Take any 2 Panels, turn so scales run in the same direction, with RS tog and stitch markers aligned, with hummus, **sl st in front and back lps** *(see Special Stitches)* in first marked st and in each st across to next marker. Fasten off. Rep with rem Panels.

Edging
Working across peaked edge, join hummus with sc in tip of first Panel, sc in same st, sc in each of next 17 sc, **sc dec** *(see Stitch Guide)* in (next sc, sl st join and first sc in next Panel), [sc in each of next 17 sc, 3 sc in next sc, sc in each of next 17 sc, sc dec in next 3 sts] 4 times, sc in each of next 17 sc, 3 sc in next sc, sc in each of next 17 sc, 2 sc in next sc, sc in each of next 217 sc, 2 sc in next sc, [sc in each of next 17 sc, 3 sc in next sc, sc in each of next 17 sc, sc dec in next 3 sts] 5 times, sc in each of next 17 sc, 3 sc in next sc, sc in each of next 17 sc, 2 sc in next sc, sc in each of next 217 sc, 2 sc in next sc, sc in each of next 17 sc, sc in first st, join in first sc. Fasten off.

Finishing
Weave in all ends. ●

STITCH GUIDE

STITCH ABBREVIATIONS

beg .... begin/begins/beginning
bpdc .... back post double crochet
bpsc .... back post single crochet
bptr .... back post treble crochet
CC .... contrasting color
ch(s) .... chain(s)
ch- .... refers to chain or space
previously made (i.e., ch-1 space)
ch sp(s) .... chain space(s)
cl(s) .... cluster(s)
cm .... centimeter(s)
dc .... double crochet (singular/plural)
dc dec .... double crochet 2 or more
stitches together, as indicated
dec .... decrease/decreases/decreasing
dtr .... double treble crochet
ext .... extended
fpdc .... front post double crochet
fpsc .... front post single crochet
fptr .... front post treble crochet
g .... gram(s)
hdc .... half double crochet
hdc dec .... half double crochet 2 or more
stitches together, as indicated
inc .... increase/increases/increasing
lp(s) .... loop(s)
MC .... main color
mm .... millimeter(s)
oz .... ounce(s)
pc .... popcorn(s)
rem .... remain/remains/remaining
rep(s) .... repeat(s)
rnd(s) .... round(s)
RS .... right side
sc .... single crochet (singular/plural)
sc dec .... single crochet 2 or more
stitches together, as indicated
sk .... skip/skipped/skipping
sl st(s) .... slip stitch(es)
sp(s) .... space(s)/spaced
st(s) .... stitch(es)
tog .... together
tr .... treble crochet
trtr .... triple treble
WS .... wrong side
yd(s) .... yard(s)
yo .... yarn over

YARN CONVERSION

OUNCES TO GRAMS		GRAMS TO OUNCES	
1	28.4	25	⅞
2	56.7	40	1⅓
3	85.0	50	1¾
4	113.4	100	3½

UNITED STATES / UNITED KINGDOM

UNITED STATES		UNITED KINGDOM
sl st (slip stitch)	=	sc (single crochet)
sc (single crochet)	=	dc (double crochet)
hdc (half double crochet)	=	htr (half treble crochet)
dc (double crochet)	=	tr (treble crochet)
tr (treble crochet)	=	dtr (double treble crochet)
dtr (double treble crochet)	=	ttr (triple treble crochet)
skip	=	miss

Single crochet decrease (sc dec): (Insert hook, yo, draw lp through) in each of the sts indicated, yo, draw through all lps on hook.

Example of 2-sc dec

Half double crochet decrease (hdc dec): (Yo, insert hook, yo, draw lp through) in each of the sts indicated, yo, draw through all lps on hook.

Example of 2-hdc dec

Reverse single crochet (reverse sc): Ch 1, sk first st, working from left to right, insert hook in next st from front to back, draw up lp on hook, yo and draw through both lps on hook.

Chain (ch): Yo, pull through lp on hook.

Single crochet (sc): Insert hook in st, yo, pull through st, yo, pull through both lps on hook.

Double crochet (dc): Yo, insert hook in st, yo, pull through st, [yo, pull through 2 lps] twice.

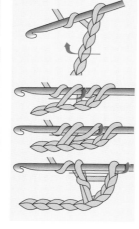

Double crochet decrease (dc dec): (Yo, insert hook, yo, draw lp through, yo, draw through 2 lps on hook) in each of the sts indicated, yo, draw through all lps on hook.

Example of 2-dc dec

Front loop (front lp) Back loop (back lp)

Front Loop   Back Loop

Front post stitch (fp): Back post stitch (bp): When working post st, insert hook from right to left around post of st on previous row.

Back   Front

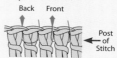

Post of Stitch

Half double crochet (hdc): Yo, insert hook in st, yo, pull through st, yo, pull through all 3 lps on hook.

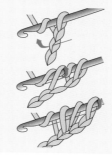

Double treble crochet (dtr): Yo 3 times, insert hook in st, yo, pull through st, [yo, pull through 2 lps] 4 times.

Treble crochet decrease (tr dec): Holding back last lp of each st, tr in each of the sts indicated, yo, pull through all lps on hook.

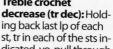

Example of 2-tr dec

Slip stitch (sl st): Insert hook in st, pull through both lps on hook.

Chain color change (ch color change) Yo with new color, draw through last lp on hook.

Double crochet color change (dc color change) Drop first color, yo with new color, draw through last 2 lps of st.

Treble crochet (tr): Yo twice, insert hook in st, yo, pull through st, [yo, pull through 2 lps] 3 times.

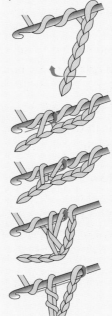

Metric Conversion Charts

METRIC CONVERSIONS

yards	x	.9144	=	metres (m)
yards	x	91.44	=	centimetres (cm)
inches	x	2.54	=	centimetres (cm)
inches	x	25.40	=	millimetres (mm)
inches	x	.0254	=	metres (m)

centimetres	x	.3937	=	inches
metres	x	1.0936	=	yards

INCHES INTO MILLIMETRES & CENTIMETRES (Rounded off slightly)

inches	mm	cm	inches	cm	inches	cm	inches	cm
1/8	3	0.3	5	12.5	21	53.5	38	96.5
1/4	6	0.6	5 1/2	14	22	56	39	99
3/8	10	1	6	15	23	58.5	40	101.5
1/2	13	1.3	7	18	24	61	41	104
5/8	15	1.5	8	20.5	25	63.5	42	106.5
3/4	20	2	9	23	26	66	43	109
7/8	22	2.2	10	25.5	27	68.5	44	112
1	25	2.5	11	28	28	71	45	114.5
1 1/4	32	3.2	12	30.5	29	73.5	46	117
1 1/2	38	3.8	13	33	30	76	47	119.5
1 3/4	45	4.5	14	35.5	31	79	48	122
2	50	5	15	38	32	81.5	49	124.5
2 1/2	65	6.5	16	40.5	33	84	50	127
3	75	7.5	17	43	34	86.5		
3 1/2	90	9	18	46	35	89		
4	100	10	19	48.5	36	91.5		
4 1/2	115	11.5	20	51	37	94		

KNITTING NEEDLES CONVERSION CHART

Canada/U.S.	0	1	2	3	4	5	6	7	8	9	10	10½	11	13	15
Metric (mm)	2	2¼	2¾	3¼	3½	3¾	4	4½	5	5½	6	6½	8	9	10

CROCHET HOOKS CONVERSION CHART

Canada/U.S.	1/B	2/C	3/D	4/E	5/F	6/G	8/H	9/I	10/J	10½/K	N
Metric (mm)	2.25	2.75	3.25	3.5	3.75	4.25	5	5.5	6	6.5	9.0

www.berroco.com

All designs in this book are made using Berroco yarn.

Annie's ® *Crocodile Stitch Afghans* is published by Annie's, 306 East Parr Road, Berne, IN 46711. Printed in USA. Copyright © 2014, 2015 Annie's. All rights reserved. This publication may not be reproduced in part or in whole without written permission from the publisher.

RETAIL STORES: If you would like to carry this publication or any other Annie's publication, visit AnniesWSL.com.

Every effort has been made to ensure that the instructions in this publication are complete and accurate. We cannot, however, take responsibility for human error, typographical mistakes or variations in individual work. Please visit AnniesCustomerService.com to check for pattern updates.

ISBN: 978-1-57367-562-8
3 4 5 6 7 8 9